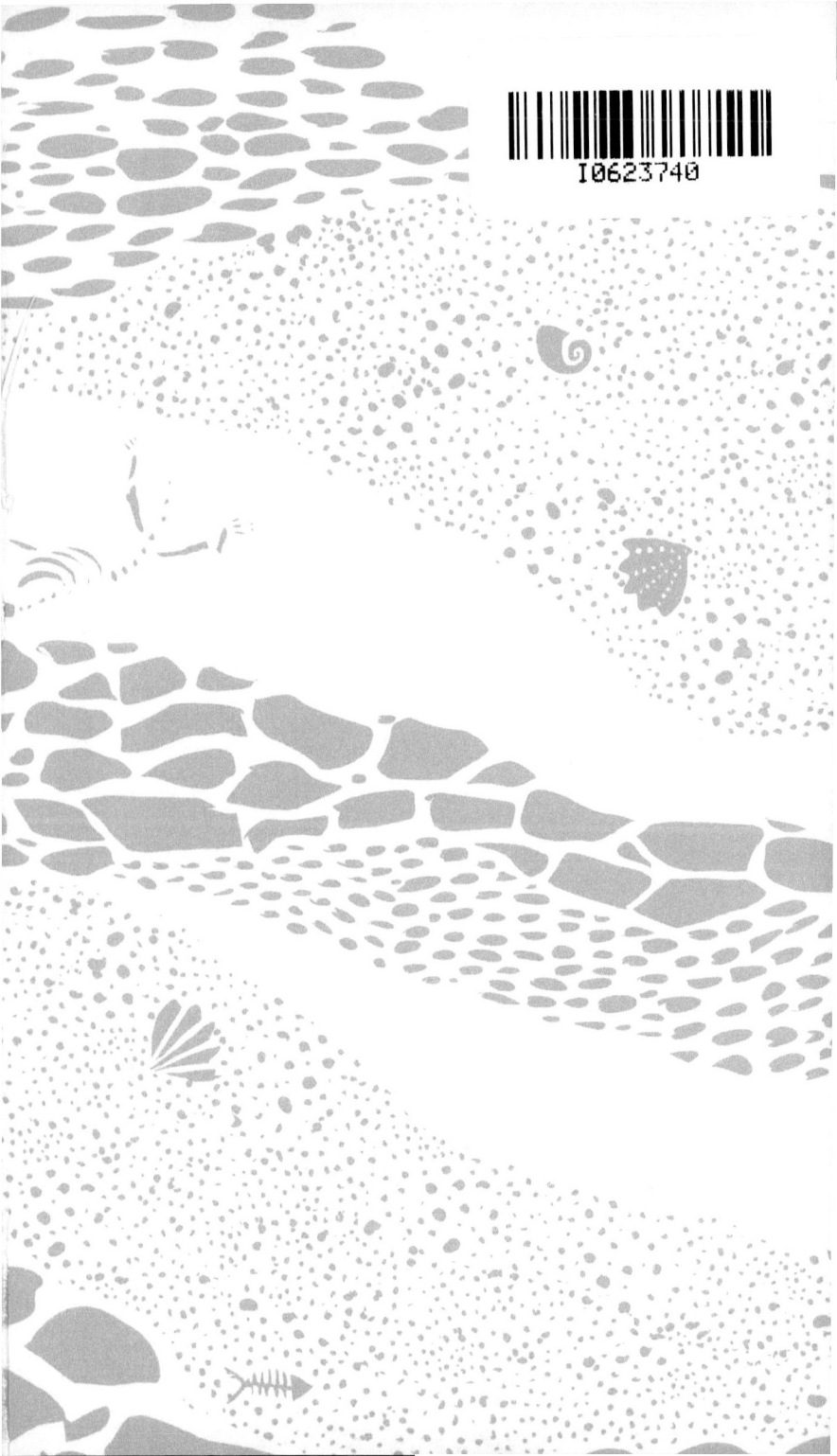

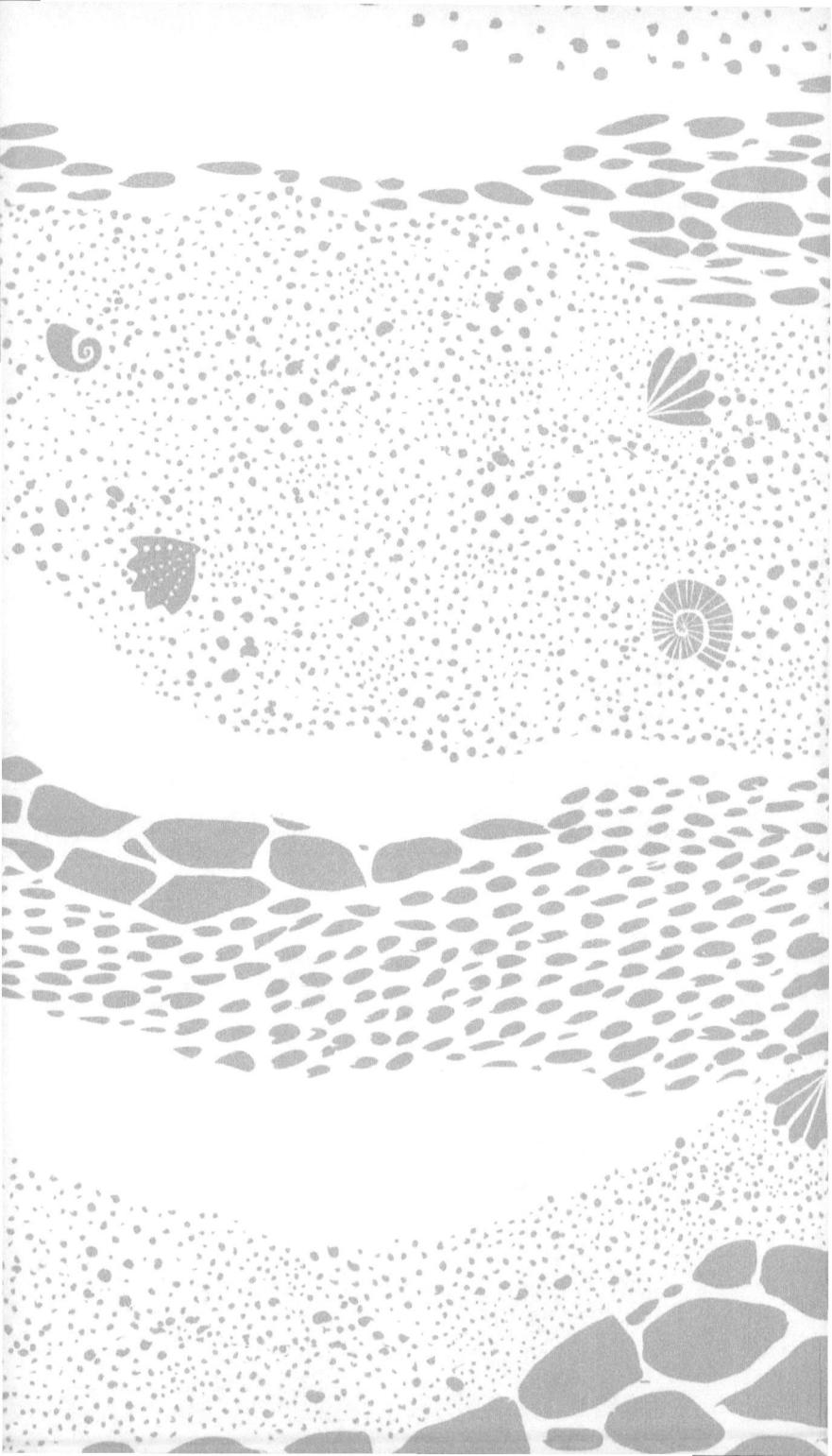

WOMB OF THE EARTH

WOMB OF THE EARTH

POEMS OF FEMINISM + ECOLOGY

RACHEL SIERRA

ISBN: 979-8-9914436-2-3

www.rachelsierraart.com
@rachel.sierra.art

Illustrations and designs by Rachel Sierra

for the sisterhood

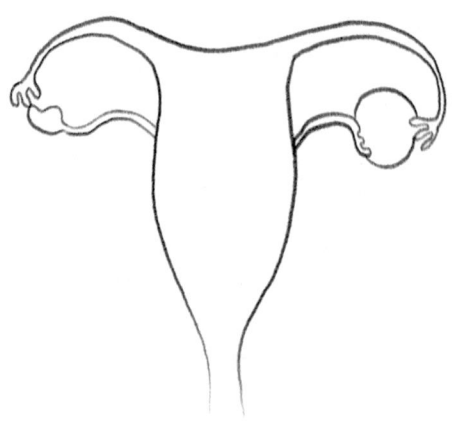

obstacle

i just
had a feeling
a *knowing*
something
wasn't right

i trust that
pain
shouldn't
be the
norm

i am
frightened

my body
is frightened

i sat
for hours
in the
waiting room

surrounded by
women

only to find out
the cat scan machine
is broken

the doctor is
late

after weeks
i have
no information
no image
no name

we are returning
to america

and i am
very aware
this option
is a
privilege

because what about them?

my soft
gentle
body
is afraid

of cutting edge
ideas

surgery

you've only
ever
healed
what's been
broken

how could
i not
love
you?

to my body

i used
to look at
you

and speak
hate

(i'm sorry)

i thought
it was
strength

to crush my
appetite
with an
iron grip

"sickly"
they said

"perfect"
i thought

daughter of the 90's

womb of the earth

i hated you
for taking up
more space

than i
felt i
deserved

to my body:

i'm sorry
i hated you.

for existing.

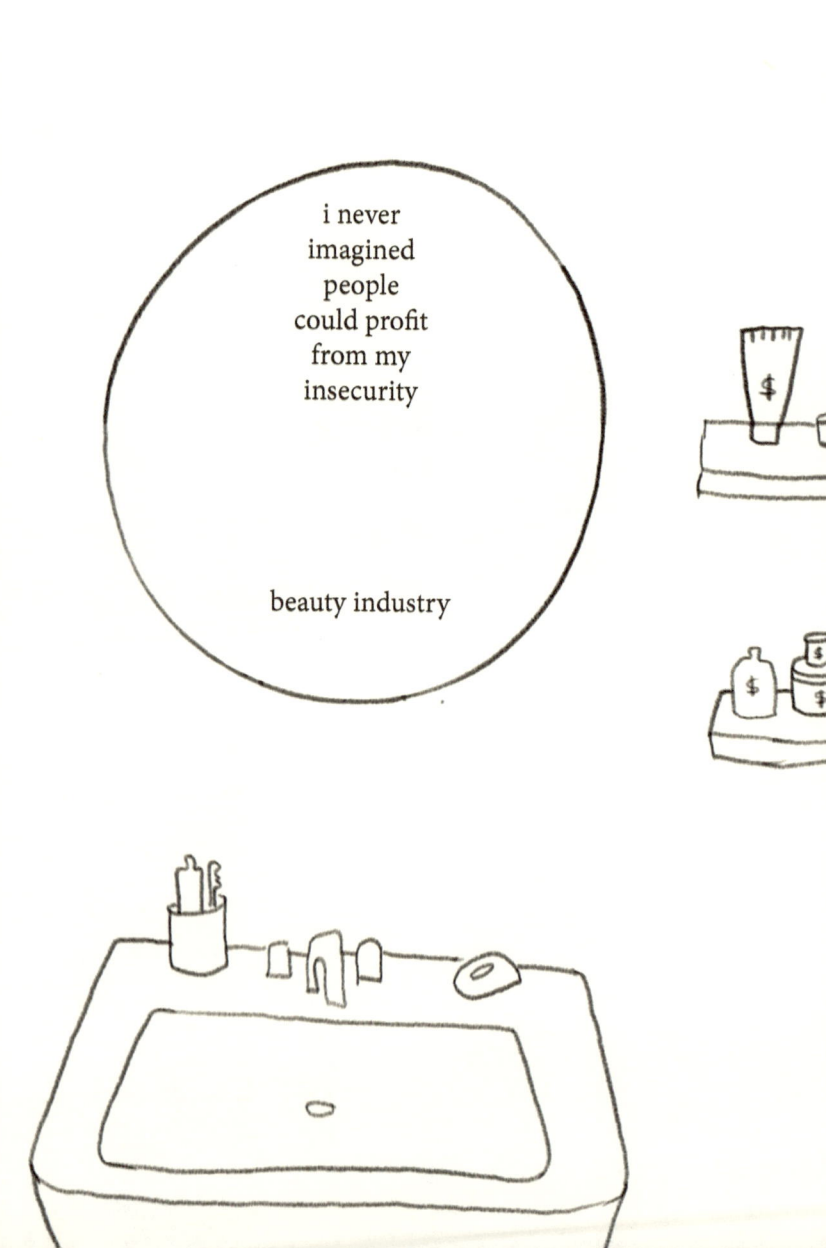

i never
imagined
people
could profit
from my
insecurity

beauty industry

to be a woman
is to restrain

appetites desires sexuality skills talent maturity size intelligence

womb of the earth

a real woman is

(overextended to the point of burnout)

a martyr

i want
to be
thin

so thin
that i
am
almost
nothing

"no,"
said my body

"we take
up space."

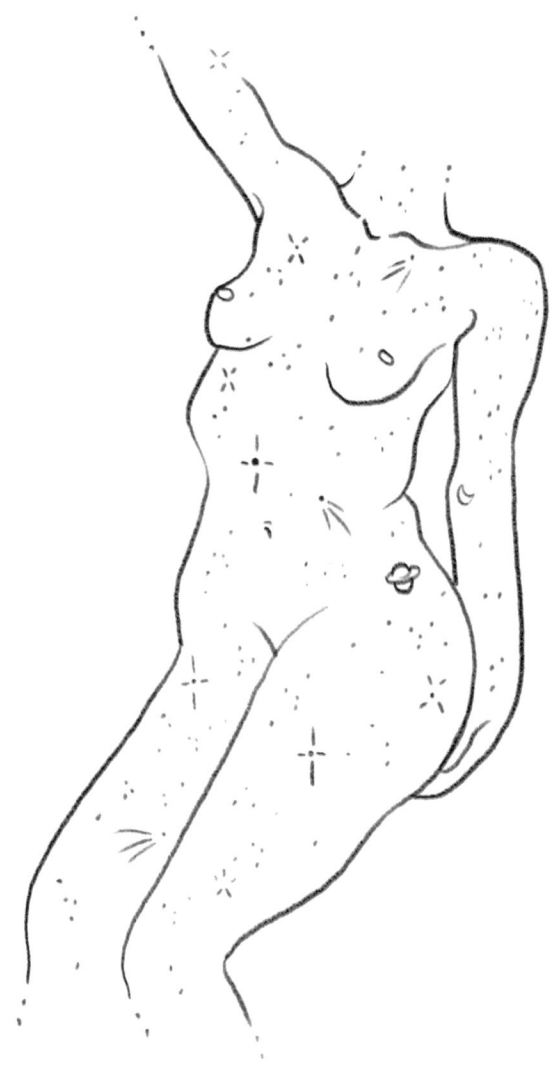

spacious

i called
you names

i called
you ugly

and all
the while

you
healed me
slowly

i couldn't
be the martyr
i wanted

my mind
was set
with pious
acceptance

but my whole body
wild with instinct

revolted

loving life
loving *this* life

it resisted
what it could not
abide

loyal, always
loyal to healing
loyal to life

she whispered
to me

"you too
can mend."

saved by my flesh

womb of the earth

my body
was my
first
resistance

womb of the earth

my body
taught
me:

thriving is revolution

i am
my own
haven

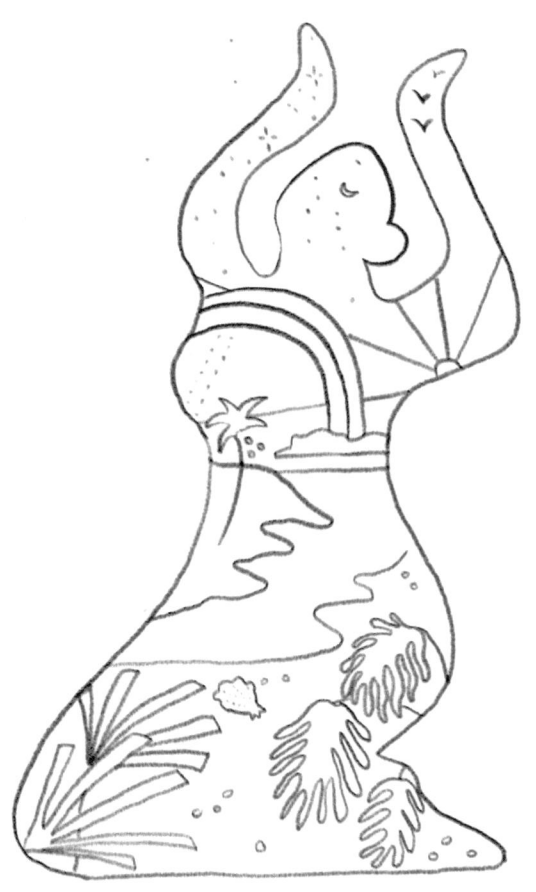

it took me
so long to
notice

how much
pain we
were in

they said
pain
was normal

so how
would i know
when it's not?

i don't know
what you
need

i'm afraid
i'm not fluent
in what
you're telling me

body language / endometriosis

just because
i am used
to this pain

doesn't mean
it is not
severe

i am not a hysterical woman

believe my pain

my uterus
does not
"weep"

crying is not
painful

(but bleeding is)

i came here
for a diagnosis

(not poetry)

why are you
not saying the
scientific words,
doctor

the only one uncomfortable (is you)

you prescribed
real hormones

as a
hypothetical solution

for a
hypothetical condition

that i
hypothetically have

and hypothetically
i do not
believe you

hypothecary

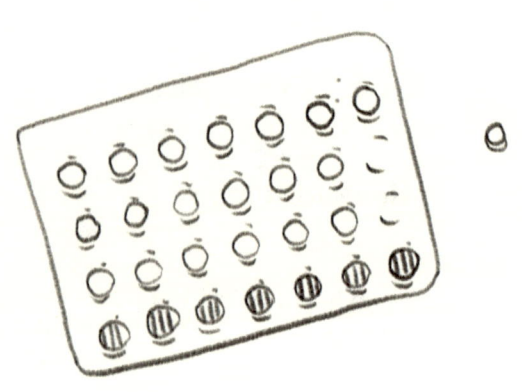

womb of the earth

the universal
band aid
for women

birth control

getting pregnant
will be
very difficult
for someone
like you

he said

but if
you do,
please consider
delivering
here

a sick sales pitch

i want to
heal me
for me

you want to
heal me
for babies

that i never
mentioned
wanting

so that
might make
you
a big ass

(-umer)

to protect
my
fertility

at the
expense
of

the quality
of life
of the one
already living

(me)

i want to heal me for me
i want to heal me for me
i want to heal me for me
i want to heal me for me
i want to heal me for me
i want to heal me for me
i want to heal me for me
i want to heal me for me
i want to heal me for me
i want to heal me for me
i want to heal me for me
i want to heal me for me
i want to heal me for me
i want to heal me for me
i want to heal me for me
i want to heal me for me
i want to heal me for me
i want to heal me for me
i want to heal me for me
i want to heal me for me
i want to heal me for me
i want to heal me for me
i want to heal me for me
i want to heal me for me
i want to heal me for me
i want to heal me for me
i want to heal me for me
i want to heal me for me
i want to heal me for me
i want to heal me for me
i want to heal me for me
i want to heal me for me
i want to heal me for me
i want to heal me for me
i want to heal me for me

holistically

womb of the earth

no caffeine
no alcohol
no gluten
no dairy
no sugar
no meat
no eggs

what is left?

54

adieu adieu

i don't
want to want
what i
cannot have

but i
already have
my baby

and this is
more than
enough

not available
for unsolicited
advice

womb of the earth

(for the rest of my life)

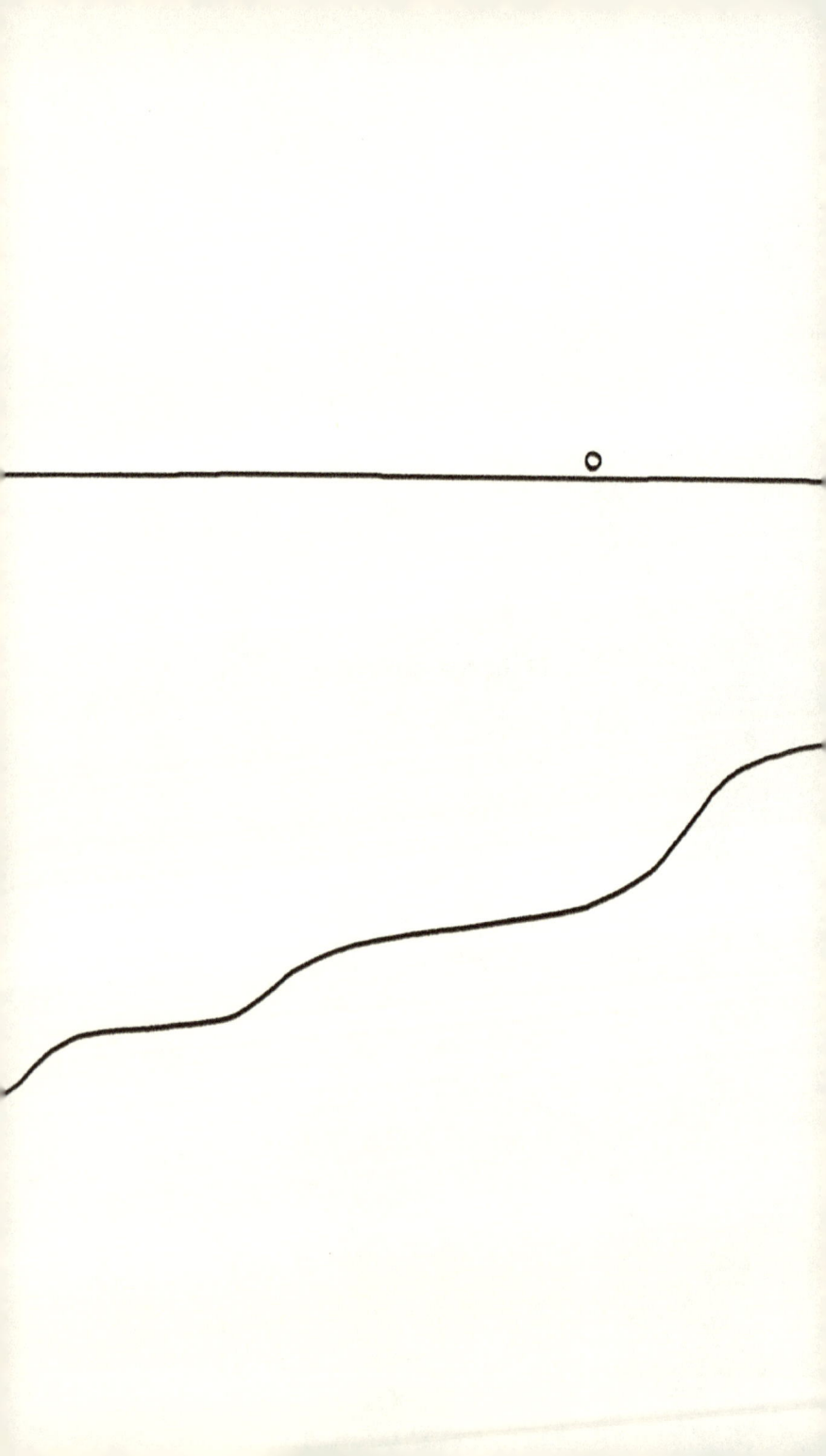

womb of the earth

a misogynist:

an emotional man
who has never
accepted
himself

(but there is still time)

please please

stop

weaponizing

your

insecurities

said the women

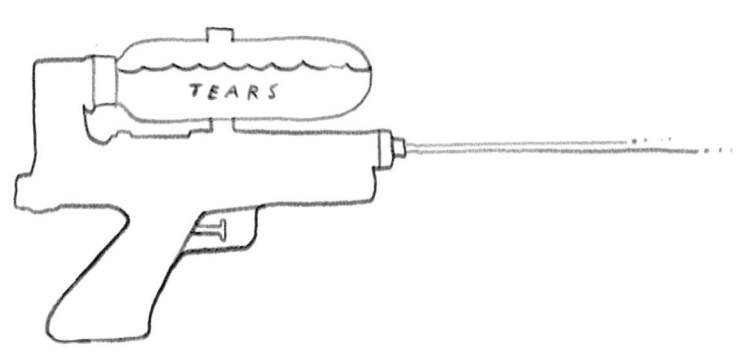

please please

stop

weaponizing

your

insecurities

said the earth

i would
apologize
but
i do not
believe
in myths

that men are
less responsible
less in control
have greater needs

or are easily
manipulated
by the wiles
of women

i do believe
though
that you have
a say in
who you
become

and you can
be responsible
for that

if you are
so threatened
by softness

so much more
than
violence

could it be

you have not
loved
yourself
properly?

the gentle man

they
strip you
of your
defenses

(and send you out)

they
will not
protect
you

and when
you are
abused

they
will not
defend
you

but they will blame you

no matter
how much
you serve them

they will
never
support you

women in the
patriarchy

you
are not
safe
there

come home

no cleavage
no bra straps
pants too low
hems too high
no tank tops
no shorts
skirts below
your knees
no bikinis
please

(your body is never appropriate)

i was
the most
reluctant
feminist

consider
how much it took
to change
that

womb of the earth

assault   robbery

stalker

fear   rapist   danger

kidnapper   predator

danger   mace

i want to
walk
alone
at night
and see
the stars

said every woman everywhere

i am a
pious
and sexy
woman

my
softness
is invincible

i can
melt
around
any one
of your
edges

vulnerability
authenticity
open mindedness
gentleness
empathy
kindness
resilience

strength

but maybe
you are
uncomfortable
with god as
she

because
you have
looked at her
and are
ashamed
of your
thoughts

accountability

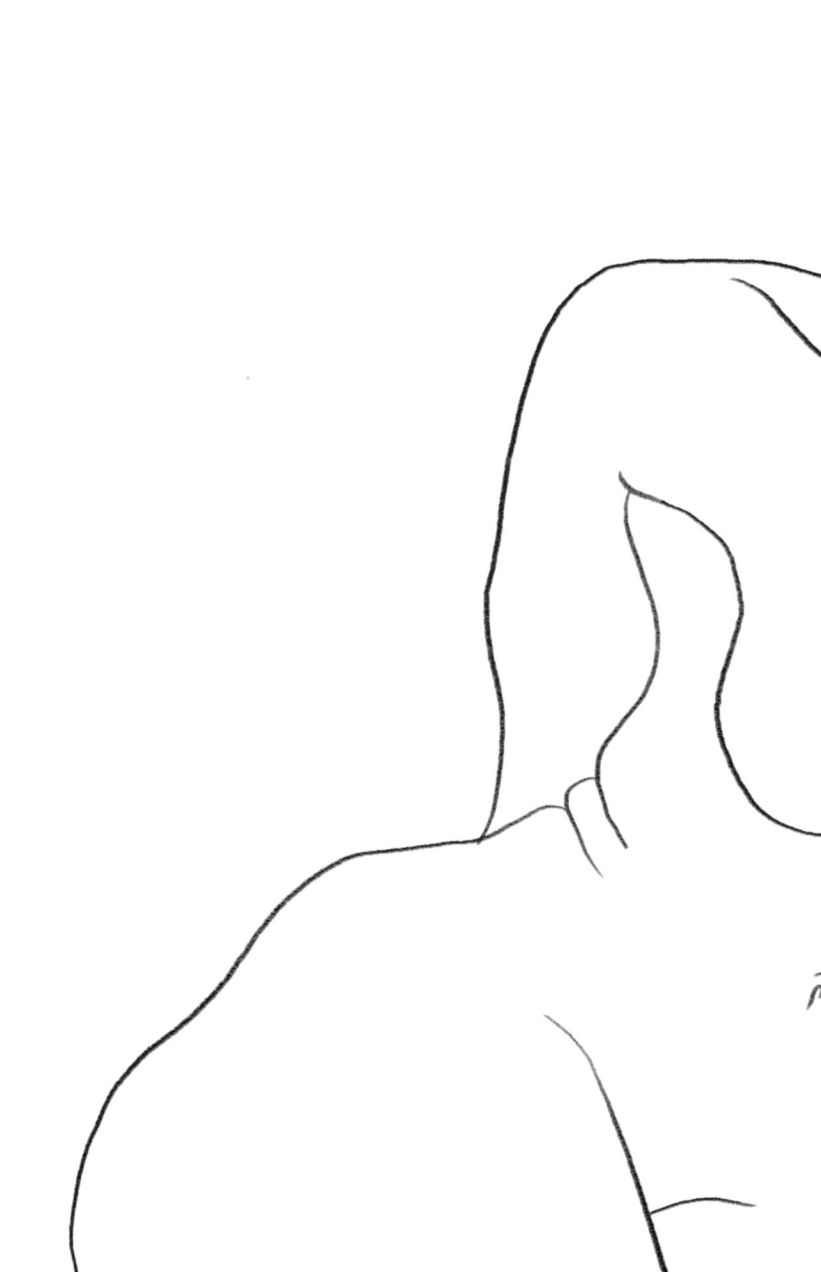

but would you
have still
embraced
jesus
if

_____

(pronoun)

were a

_____

(gender)

?

an unbiased question

because
if god
became
human

they could
have
become
any
one
of us:

female
black
lgbtq+
brown
them
him
etc.

options

if it is not
good news

for all of us

then it
is not
good

gospel

the mother's prayer

our mother
who art
in the cosmos
sacred is
thy name

may your
children
hear your voice
and return to your
ever loving embrace

give us this day
nourishment
from your
body, spirit,
and lands

teach us to
walk lightly
upon this
generous and
nurturing earth

heal our
self inflicted wounds
and absorb
our offenses
in your profound empathy

forgive us when
we forget the beauty
of who we truly are
may we strive to see
the truest self in one another

may we be
healers
peacemakers
and empaths
in return

as you fiercely
protect us
may we
resiliently
defend

the vulnerable,
the marginalized,
and the oppressed
with nonviolence
as we see you do

amen

oh my
sweet
mother

who was
not
mothered

i long
to
remother
you

i recognize
this

said my
body

i have
dwelt here
before

my mother's embrace

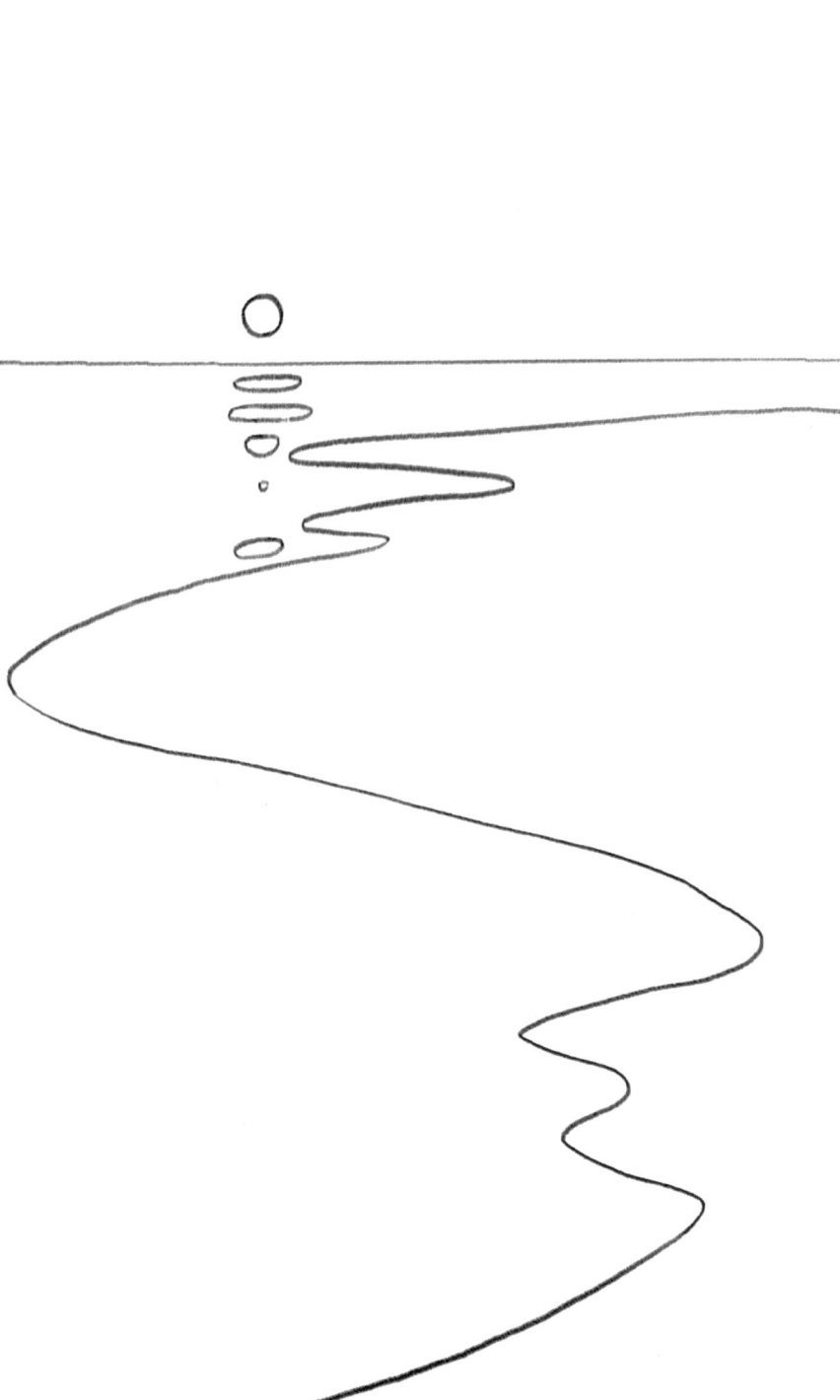

it is hard
to have
boundaries
with a mother

once we
shared
all of our
borders

you
also included
me

and even now
your emotions
still pull
at my tides

my great
grandmother
was seventy seven
when she
divorced
her abusive
husband

though i didn't
know her
for very long

she showed me:

it's never
too late
to love
yourself

a triumph

womb of the earth

boundaries are for me
boundaries are for me
boundaries are for me
boundaries are for me
boundaries are for me

it is an
opportunity
to love
myself
relentlessly

i do not
believe
there are
hysterical
women

i believe
women
who have
never
been heard
will raise
their
voices

chorus

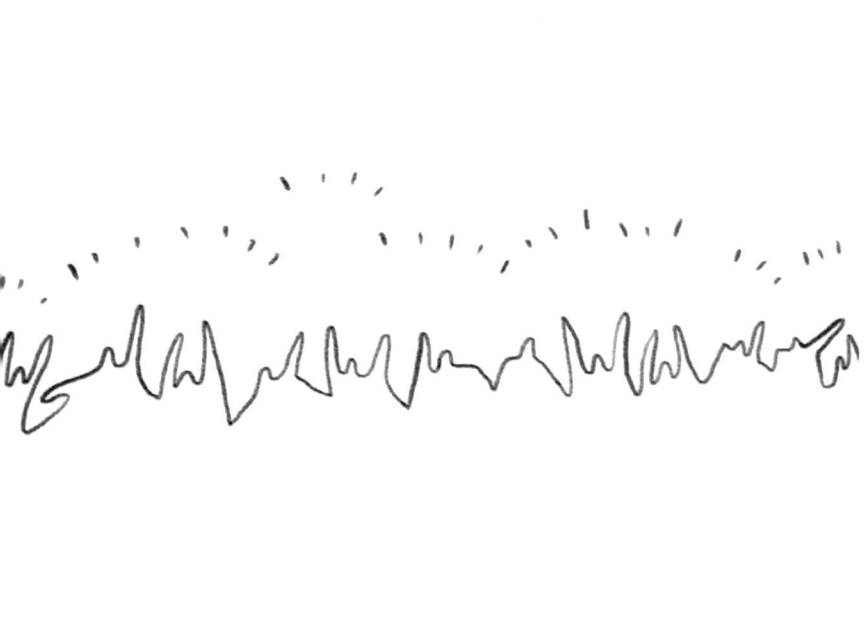

womb of the earth

comparison

is what
they
do to us
out there

it is
safe
in here

sisterhood

sister
sister

you have
gotten lost

come home
to yourself

come home

to us

follow our voices

womb of the earth

i seek out
a sisterhood

wherever
i may
go

coven

follow your
joy

follow your
love

it is the
doorway

enter
into your
mystery

descend
to your
depth

and once
you find it

don't
let go

i tried
to be
for you

everything
i ever
needed

but now
you must be
everything
for yourself

little sister love yourself

i don't want
to be
your rival

i am
better
with you
by my
side

~~competition~~ collaboration

if they
feel
themselves
dimmed
by your light

remember
remember

you are
only
lighting
your own
path

and showing them the way

honey

no one
else's
value

lessens your own

but i tell you,

together
you are
exponential

womb of the earth

someone
benefits
from pitting us
against
each other

(you are not my enemy)

if you aren't
getting your
needs met

and neither
am i

maybe

there is a
problem
with this
system

no such thing as red or blue

the american
dream,
or just another
prosperity gospel

preaching the
cruel ideology that
only the honest
only the hardworking
only the good
deserve to thrive

but when the good suffer,
the corrupt excel,
when there is
no one to turn to

won't we wake
one another
gently

with soft sounds like

"i'm here" and
"you're safe now" and
"it was only just a dream"

and when
you say

god bless america

do you
mean

and everywhere else

or is there
a small quiet
prayer of

and nowhere else

hidden in the
blank spaces

what a parched
and brittle
little prayer

when the
earth beneath
your feet

flourishes
without
exception

who decided
to carve up this land

piercing it
with dotted lines
indelible on maps
but invisible to the eye

where did we
get the idea
to claim it

we cannot
own
the earth
for she already
belongs to
herself

how could we
see her as anything
but a gift

for the only life
we could
ever own
is our own

the earth
belongs
to herself
alone

we must
learn
to share her
equally

if you
don't care
about the earth

won't you at least
do something
to save yourself?

our fates are
intertwined

and no matter
what language
i'm speaking

it doesn't seem
to translate:

*we need
each other
to survive*

if we
are not
contributing
to the
ecosystem

taking and
not giving

we are
by definition
a virus

we are
also
mammals

we are
endemic
to this
earth

our habitat
our home

and losing our
ecosystem is
also
traumatic

earthlings

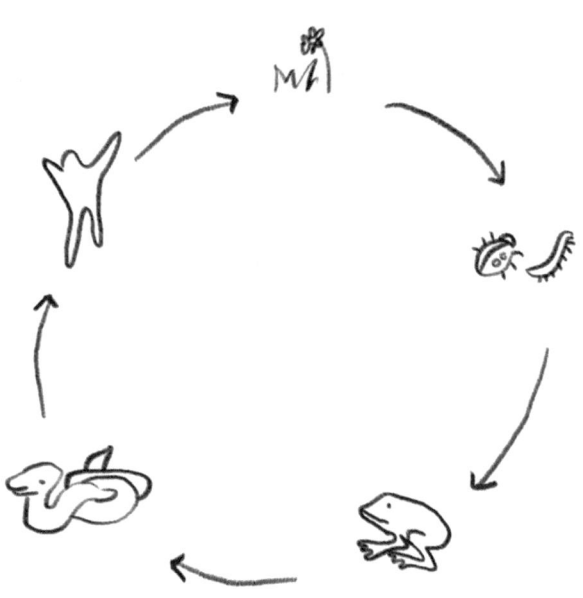

let's not forget
capitalism
was built
by the labor
of the oppressed

it is not
a fair or just
system

when
there are
many things
to tip the
scales

systemic inequality

there is no such thing
as cheap labor

all life is priceless

(you are priceless)

and cannot be
sliced into
lengths of time
in exchange
for
money

womb of the earth

that slippery
thing
always just
out of reach

want

we have been
conditioned
to consume

and it is
poisoning
our earth
our reefs
our seas
our forests
our bees

but can't you see
we are also
killing ourselves
slowly

how to cure
this
epidemic
of want

because i
also want

i want this earth to survive us

lay down your
profit margins
and
follow me

jesus was no capitalist

take a pause
from
participating
in the
endless exchange
of the
global economy

sabbath

all of the
money on earth
cannot buy
one single life

existence is a
miracle

it cannot be traded
cannot be bought

it can only
be lived

rest is a revolution

you are
more

than a

producer / consumer

rest + let rest

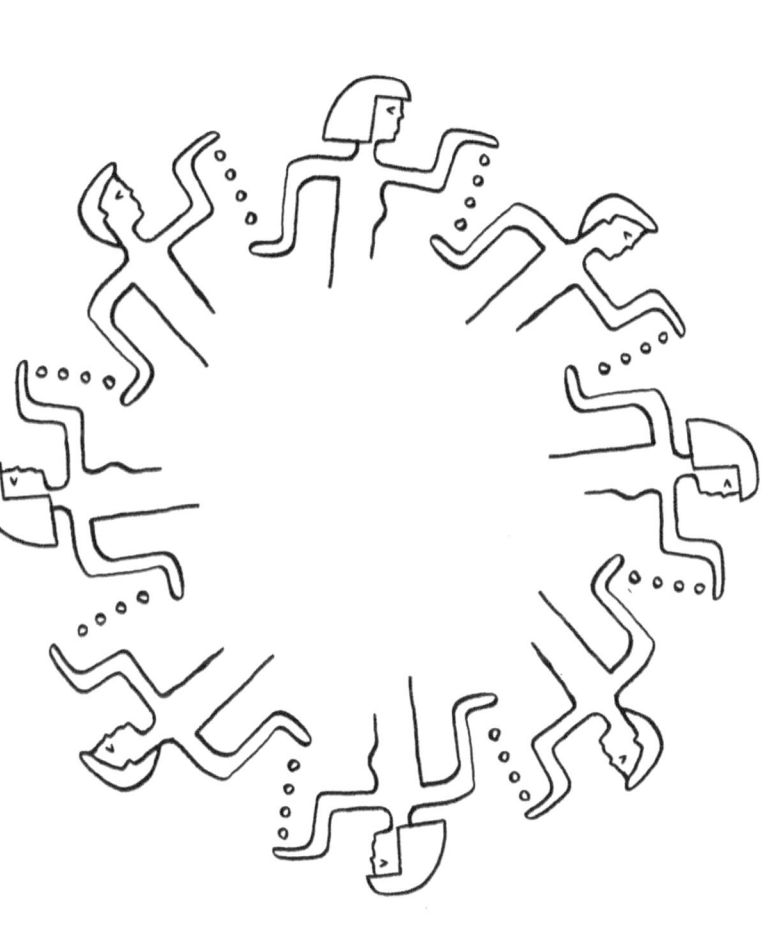

but
if everyone
rested

could it be

everyone
would have
enough

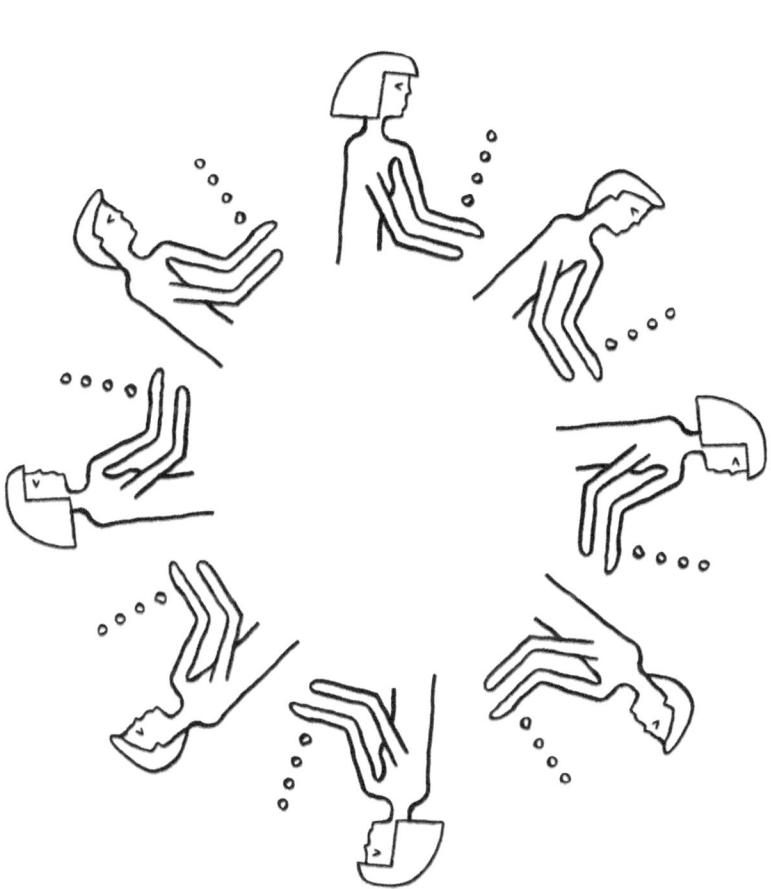

you cannot
measure my worth
by how much
i
produce

productivity ≠ value

you cannot
measure my worth
by how much
i
(re) produce

fertility ≠ value

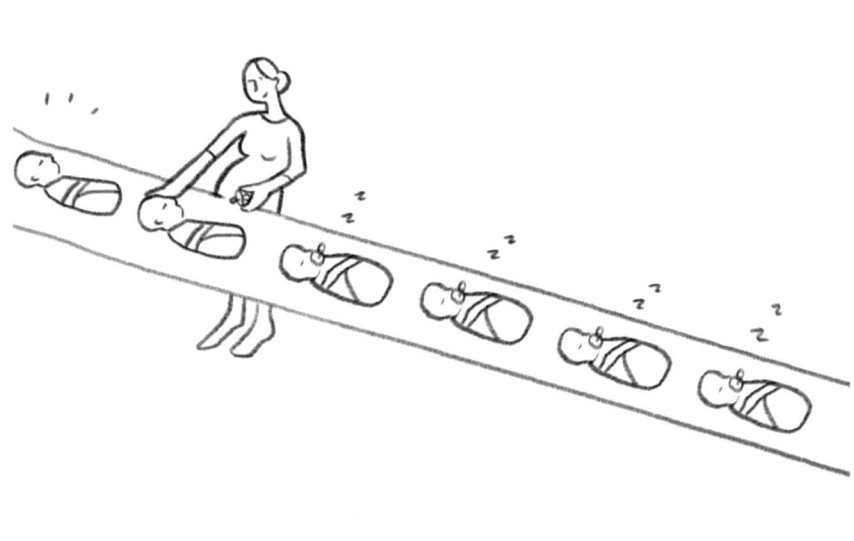

i know you
care
about the
unborn

but
what about
caring

just as much

for people
who are
already
living

the displaced the homeless the immigrants
the refugees the orphans the oppressed
the gangsters the criminals the addicts
the healthy the sick the young the old
the rich the poor the middle class
yes, also the babies

but do you
only value
my life
because
i can
create
new life

womb of the earth

it seems
it costs
an entire life

to make
a new
one

(and i like my life)

maybe i have had
too much
demanded
from me

i do
not want
to share

i do not
want
to tear my body
in two
for someone else

isn't it enough
to simply be

(me)

womb of the earth

stop asking
stop asking
stop asking
stop asking

engagement marriage pregnancy kids

and if
one day
i do

(become a mother)

i feel
somewhat
betrayed

by my own body

to fill me
with so many
hormones

that i cannot help
but love
my captor

a stuck home syndrome

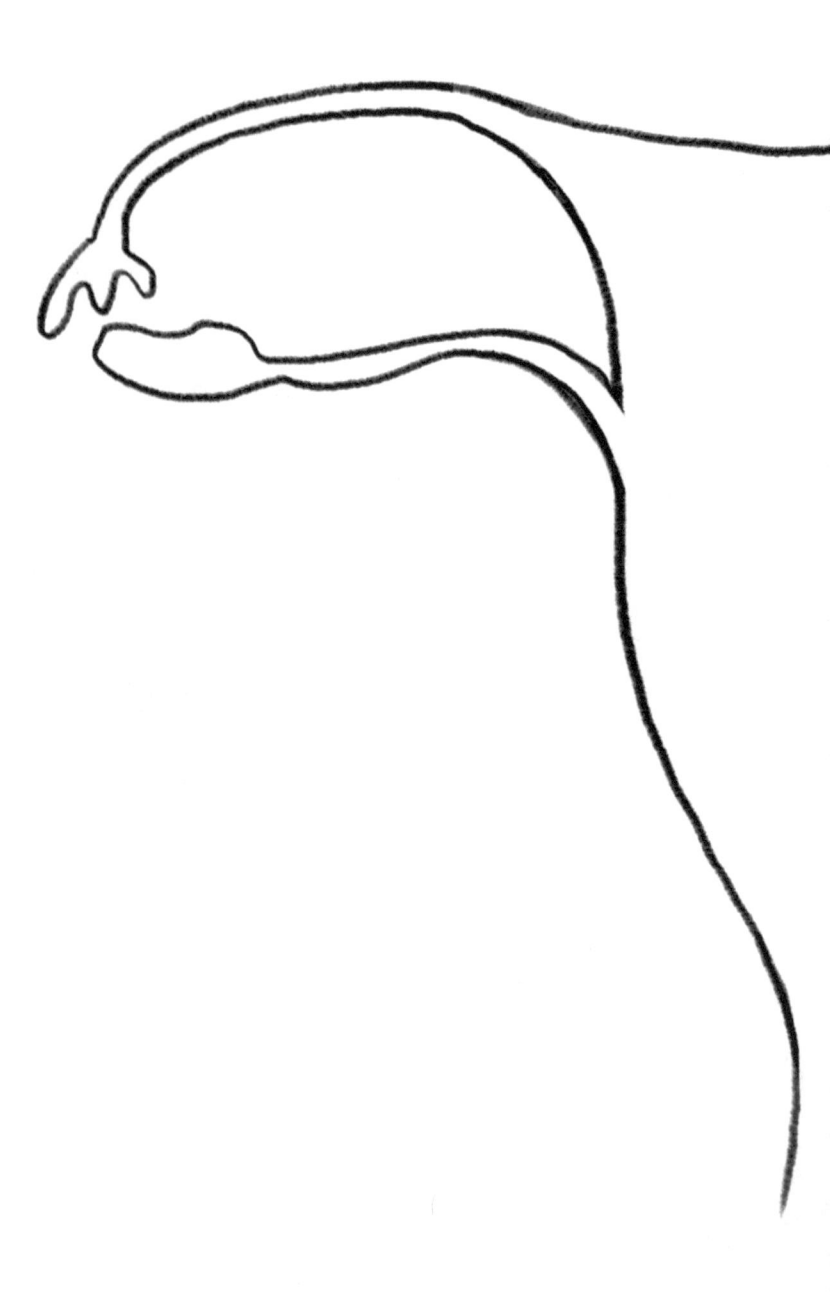

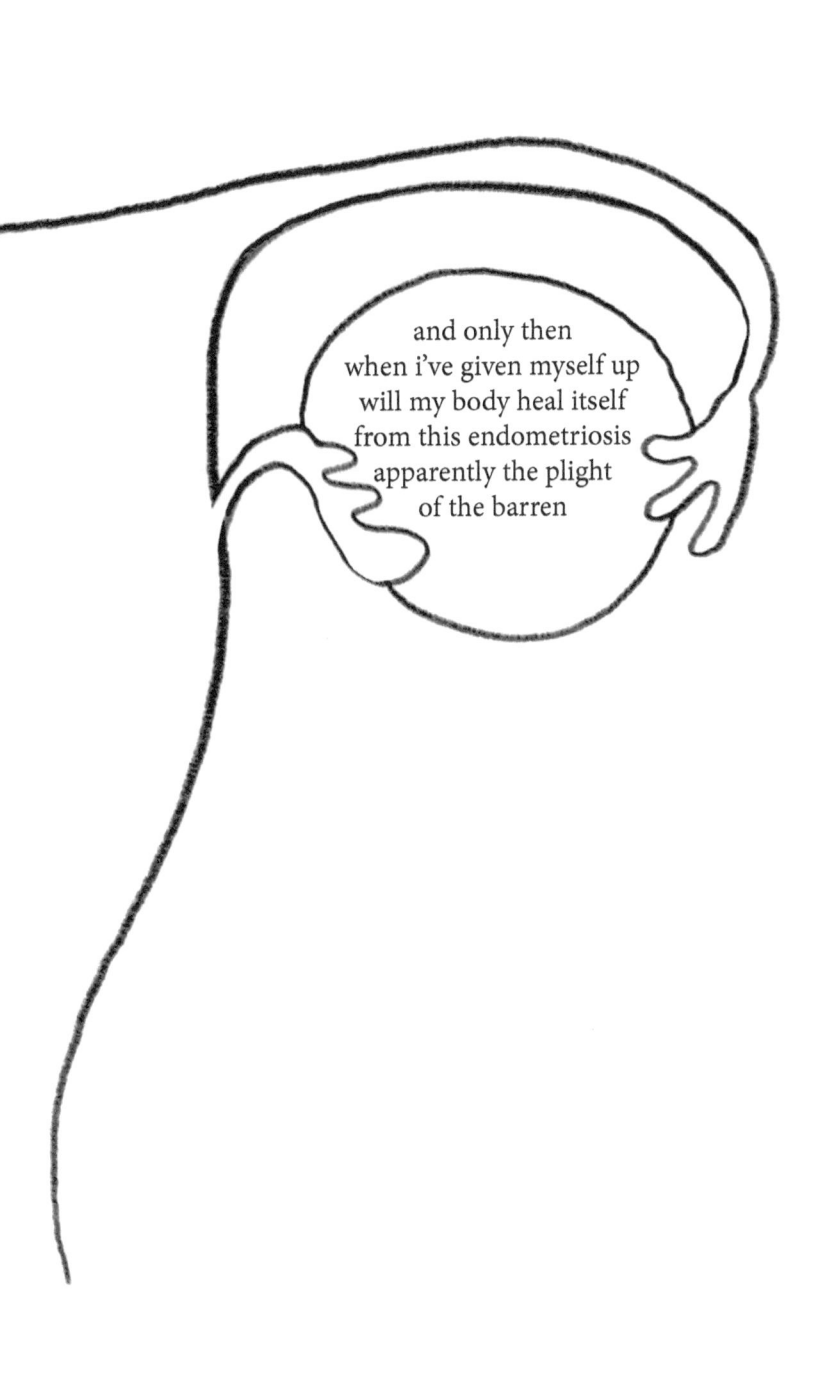

and only then
when i've given myself up
will my body heal itself
from this endometriosis
apparently the plight
of the barren

but how
do i
step into
the joy
of my life?

the one not
an endless
chain of reactions

i am angry,
so how to heal?

or better yet,
how to lock
the door

think what
you will,
out there

you are not
welcome
here

my sacred space
my holy place

the weight
of their
expectation
is heavy

and it is
not mine
to hold

so i lay down
what they
set upon me

and i walk
onward
on my
path

maybe the strongest thing i'll ever do

is to be wholly for myself

to be whole for myself alone

you belong
to yourself

before

you belong
to
anyone
else

i have been
dreaming of

flower infusions
scented oils
spices

and shells,
everywhere

glossy
pearly
giant

if you could
dream
your own
cure

could your
healing
be this
lovely?

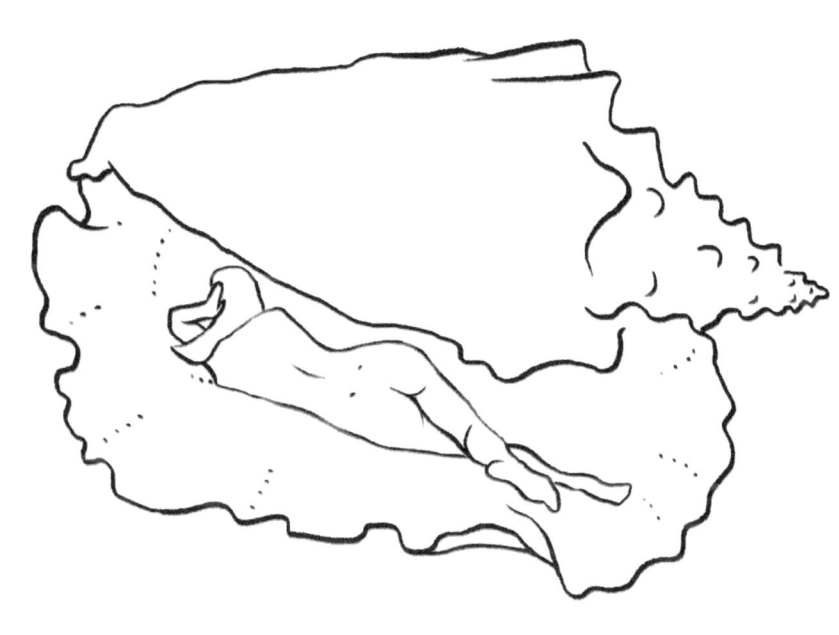

i believe
i can
heal myself

if i listen
closely
enough

but like
the earth
she whispers

breezing gently

but she will
shout
if she must

fires rage
floods sweep
and the earth quakes
with the rage
of not being heard

i want us
to dream
our way

into a
new way
of being

~~anthropocentrism~~ ecocentrism

i don't want to
simply exist

i want to be
an overgrowth
so obstinately thriving

a wilderness
to be reckoned with
thorny and sweet

as fresh as rushing rivers
and rained soaked soil

irresistible as
fragrant petals
in the hot humid night

blooming like the moon
pressing back the darkness
with her luscious light

and like the mosses
giving more than i take

i will gladly
give myself back
to this dark scented earth

like sand falls
between my fingers
and is embraced
back into everything

slow down, buy better, own less,
make more, dream bigger, waste little,
give away, choose used, grow food,
compost, rest, disconnect, reuse,
borrow, share, trade, repair

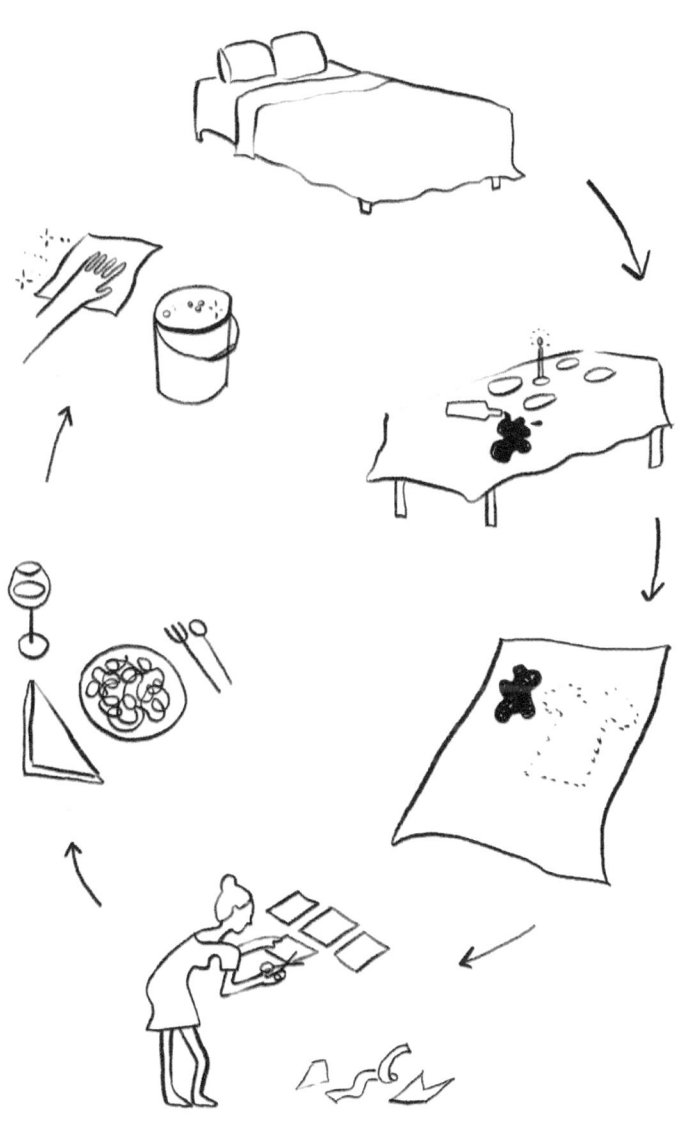

a man
is
an island

but a woman
is
an emergent piece
of subcontinental land
surrounded
by water

and connected
to
everything

grounded

how we treat women
is
how we treat the earth
is
how we treat women
is
how we treat the earth
is
how we treat women
is
how we treat the earth
is
how we treat women
is
how we treat the earth
is
how we treat women
is
how we treat the earth
is
how we treat women
is
how we treat the earth
is
how we treat women
is
how we treat the earth
is
how we treat women
is
how we treat the earth

how we heal women
is
how we heal the earth
is
how we heal women
is
how we heal the earth
is
how we heal women
is
how we heal the earth
is
how we heal women
is
how we heal the earth
is
how we heal women
is
how we heal the earth
is
how we heal women
is
how we heal the earth
is
how we heal women
is
how we heal the earth
is
how we heal women
is
how we heal the earth

womb of the earth

please

STOP

exploiting me for my resources

said the women

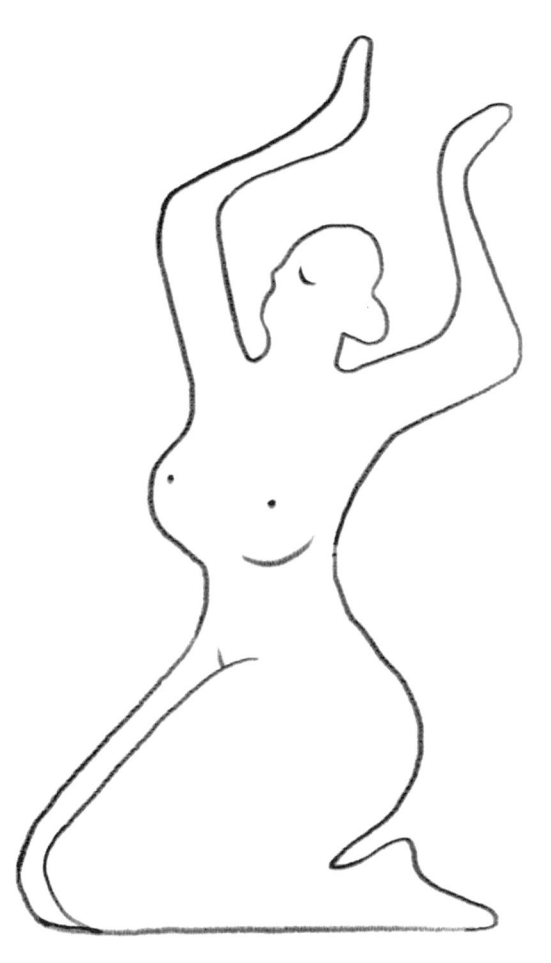

womb of the earth

please

STOP

exploiting me for my resources

said the earth

give me
autonomy
and
let me
rest

i know
how to
heal
myself

said the women

give me
autonomy
and
let me
rest

i know
how to
heal
myself

said the earth

every morning
when the light
touches
this land

i feel an almost
painful love
for this place

this place

there is no
other

when i walk
i cannot help
but feel
every leaf
brushing me

as a caress

every scented flower
a gift

every fallen fruit
a token

of this wild
abundant
love

womb of the earth

when i lay
on the sand
embraced by
sunlight

why do i feel
lifted
held
so tenderly?

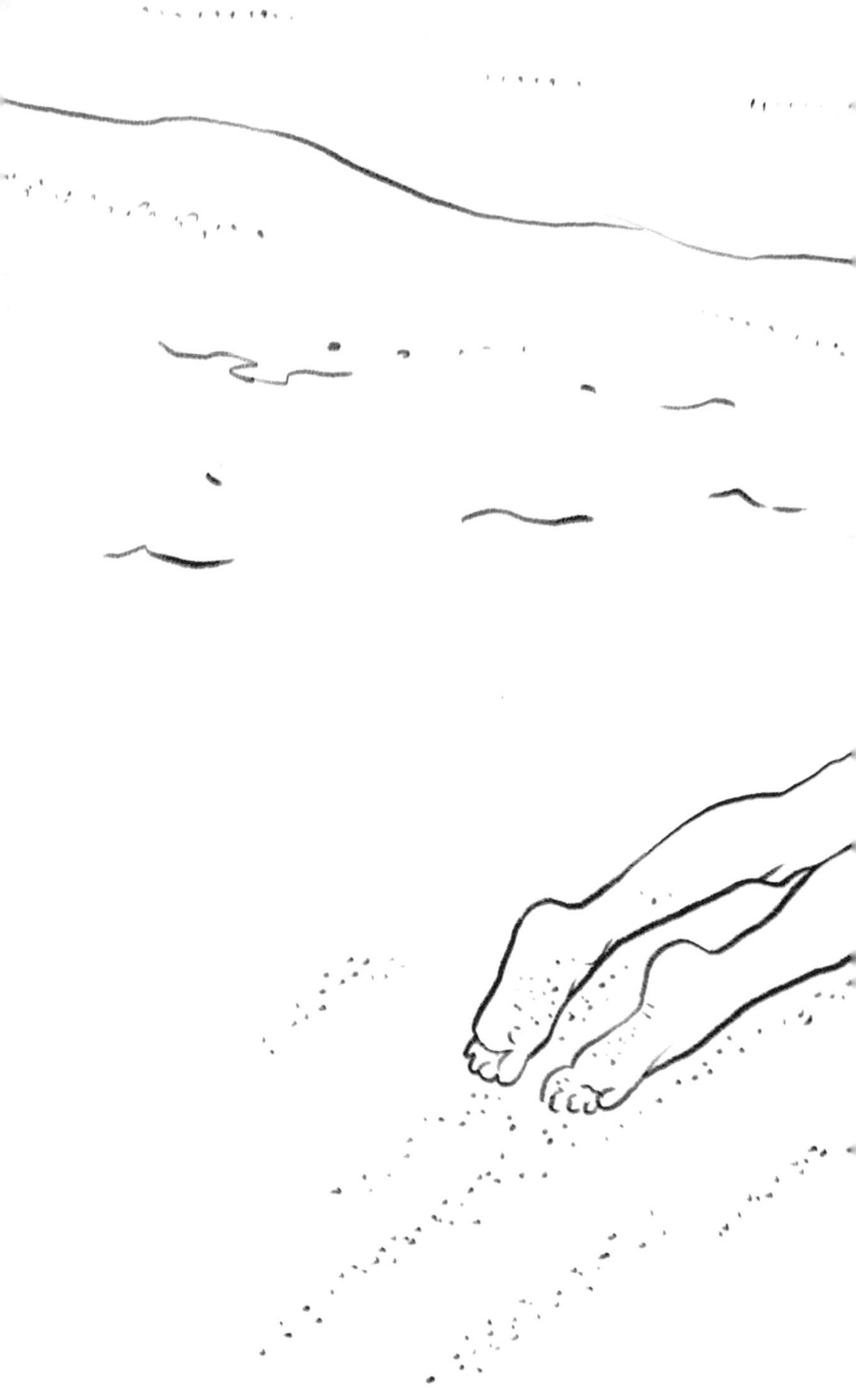

i don't want to take
from this earth

i want to sow seeds

i want to know
every leaf by name

i want to be worthy
of this wild love

the earth precedes us

our elemental
mother

may we walk
with care

scattering seeds
in our footsteps

leaving
no trace

and if one day
nobody remembers

may it be
a breath of peace

a love song
to you

magical, this

holding the
elements of
billions of years
of history

also,
holding
the elements
to endlessly
create our future

everyone and everything
is here

in the palm
of my hand

soil

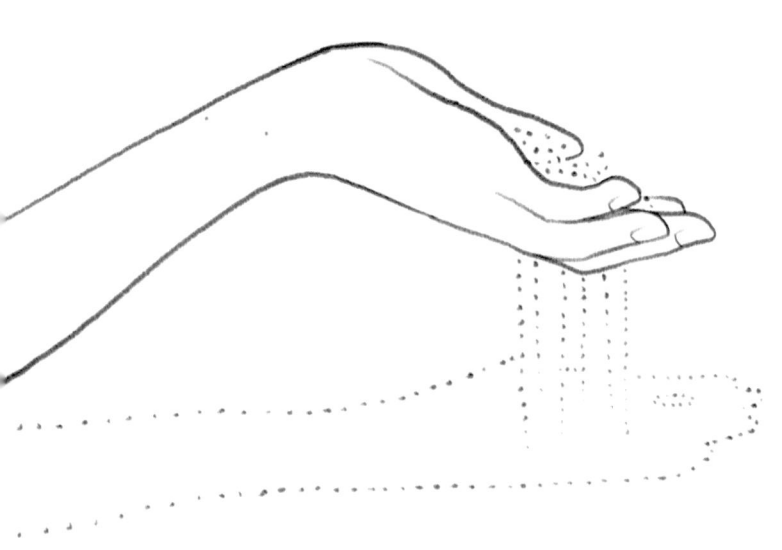

magical, this

holding the
elements of
billions of years
of my ancestry

also,
holding
the elements
to endlessly
create our future

everyone and everything
is here

in the
cells of my
living being

appreciate
the me who i was
to be the me who i am
and become the me who i will be

remember
your way
back to
yourself

you,

who you have
always been

and who you
are yet
to become

womb of the earth

my
body
is
of
the
earth

and my soul is fertile soil

find your
courage

find your
voice

find your
power

find your joy

womb of the earth

who you are

is

who you were

always

meant to become

curada

may you
rewild
yourself

decaying
blossoming
and fruiting
cyclically

may you give
more than you
receive

balanced and
flourishing
con
amor y tiempo

may you be
lush and abundant

may you be
just like
your mother

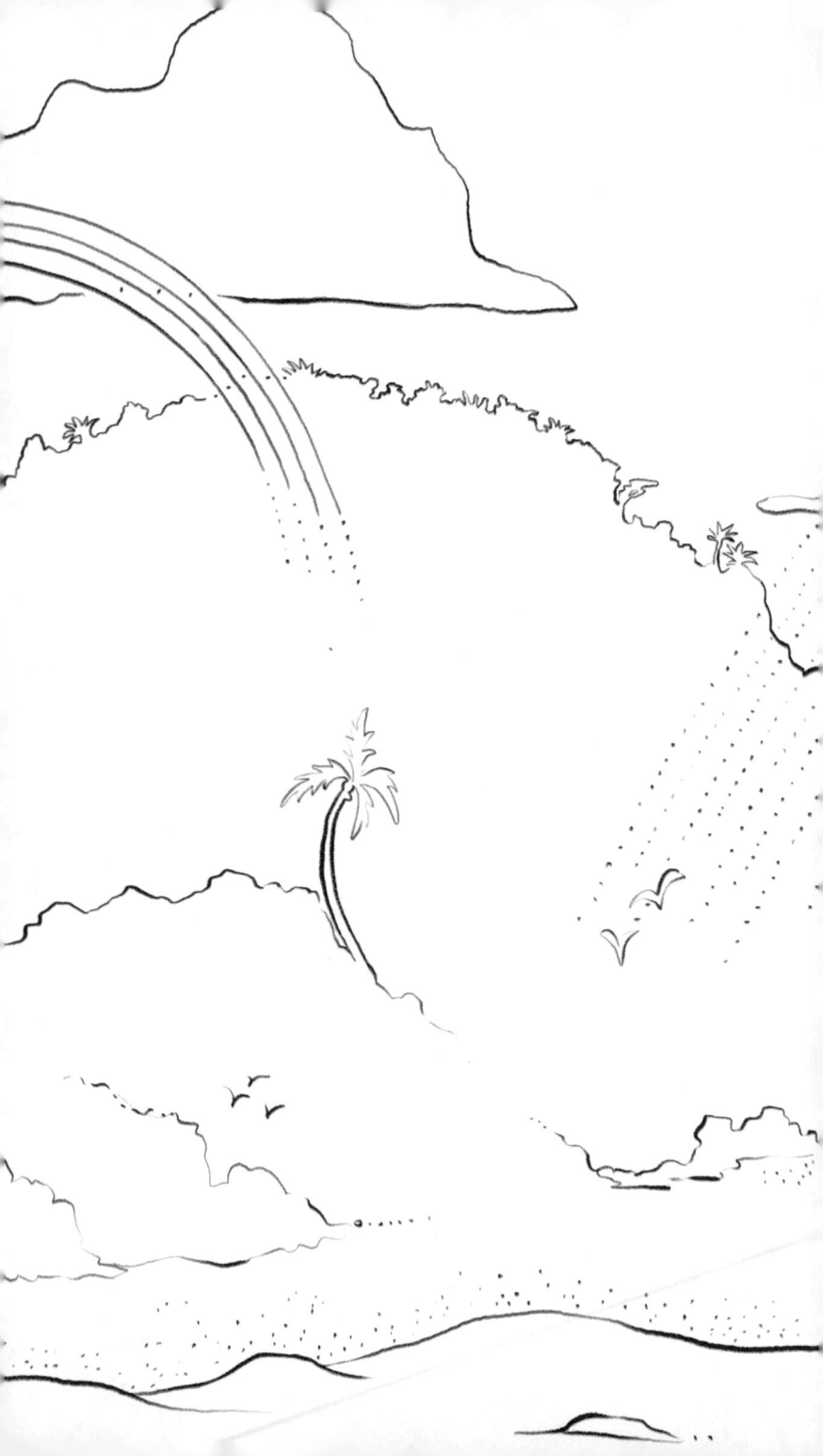

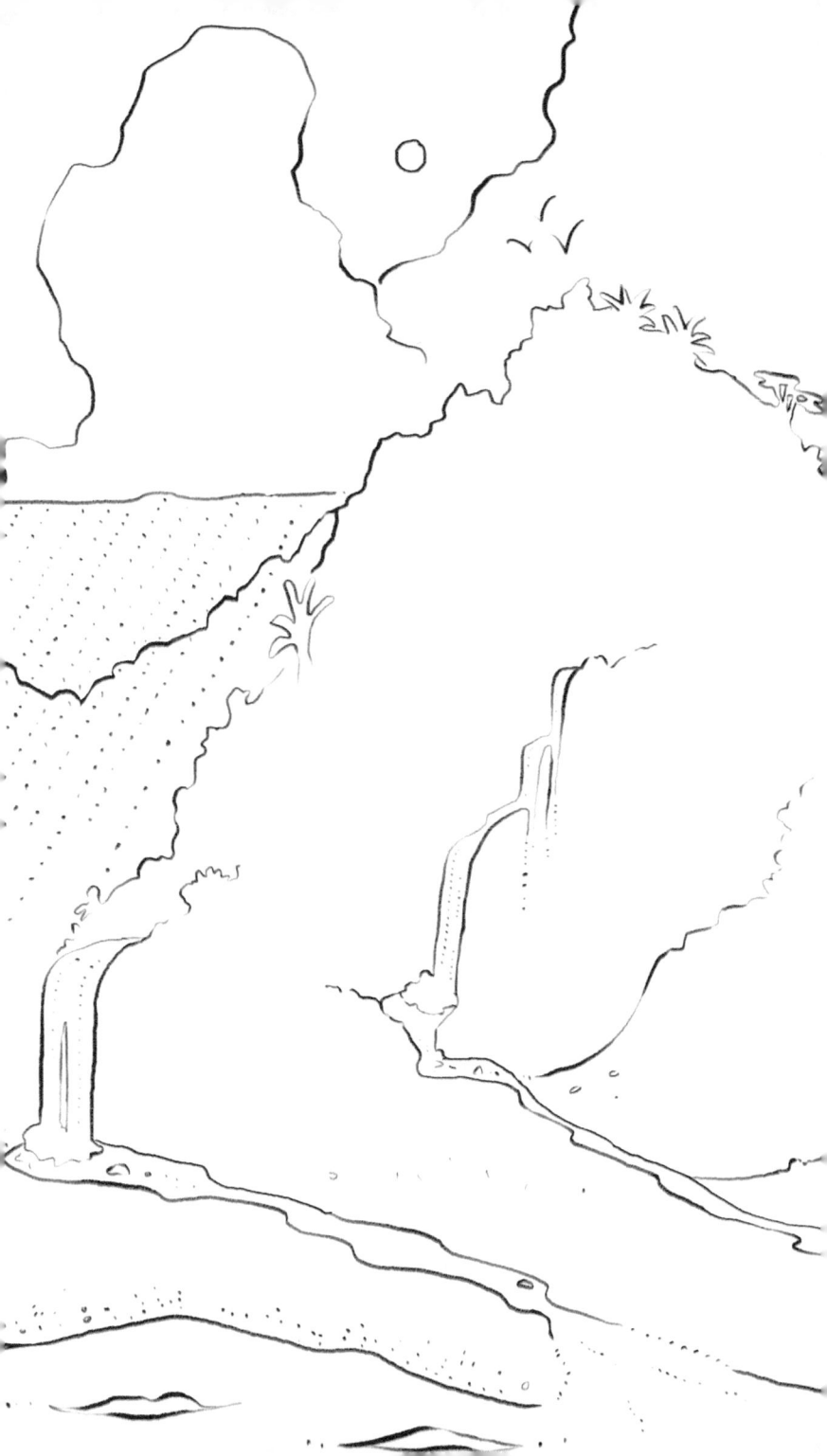

About the Author

Rachel Sierra grew up in the Caribbean and South America, and travel has been a central part of her life. As a self-taught painter and multidisciplinary creative, her work has been displayed in galleries and in print internationally. When she's not painting in her studio, you'll find her surfing, diving, or otherwise outside. She is driven to document life in any way - whether by painting, film photography, or writing poetry.

R A C H E L S I E R R A A R T . C O M

@rachel.sierra.art